DATE DUE

CONTINENTS

South America

Mary Virginia Fox

Heinemann Library
Chicago, Illinois

Designed by Joanna Hinton-Malivoire and Q2A Creative
Printed in China by South China Printing Company

10 09 08 07 06
10 9 8 7 6 5 4 3 2 1

New edition ISBN: 1-4034-8545-3 (hardcover)
              1-4034-8553-4 (paperback)

The Library of Congress has cataloged the first edition as follows:
Fox, Mary Virginia.
        South America / Mary Virginia Fox.
                p. cm. – (Continents)
        Includes bibliographical references and index.
        ISBN 1-58810-002-2
        1. South America –Juvenile literature. [2. South
America.] – Geography – Juvenile literature. I.Title. II. Continents
(Chicago, Ill.)
F2208.5 .F695 2001
980–dc21   00-011470

Acknowledgments
The publishers are grateful to the following for permission to reproduce copyright material: Earth Scenes/Fabio Colonbini, p. 5; Photo Edit/E. Zuckerman, p. 6; Earth Scenes/Breck P. Kent, pp. 9, 19; Tony Stone/Kevin Schafer, p. 11; Corbis/Adam Woolfitt, p. 13; Brian Vikander, p. 14; Animals Animals/Partridge, p. 15; Earth Scenes, p. 16; DDB Stock Photo/ Robert Fried, p. 21; Tony Stone/Avenida Paulista, p. 22; Peter Arnold/Jeff Greenberg, Inc., p. 23; Earth Scenes/Nigel J. H. Smith, p. 24; Earth Scenes/Michael Fogden, p. 25; Bruce Coleman/Timothy O'Keefe, Inc., p. 27; Tony Stone/Ary Diesendruck, p. 28; Photo Researchers/Georg Gerster, p. 29.

Cover photograph of South America, reproduced with permission of Science Photo Library/ Tom Van Sant, Geosphere Project/ Planetary Visions.

The publishers would like to thank Kathy Peltan, Keith Lye, and Nancy Harris for their assistance in the preparation of this book.

Every effort has been made to contact copyright holders of any material reproduced in this book. Any omissions will be rectified in subsequent printings if notice is given to the publisher.

Some words are shown in bold, **like this**. You can find out what they mean by looking in the glossary.

Contents

Where Is South America?

A continent is a very large area of land. There are seven continents in the world. South America is one of them. A narrow strip of land connects South America to the continent of North America.

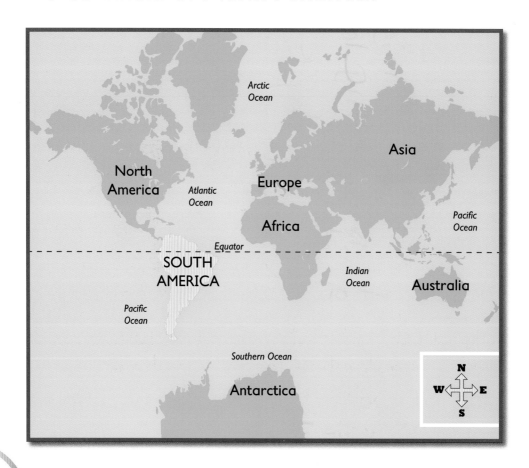

▲ *Brazil's Atlantic coast has sandy beaches.*

South America is almost completely surrounded by oceans. The Pacific Ocean is to the west. The Atlantic Ocean is to the east. Most of South America is below the **Equator**. The Equator is an imaginary line around the center of Earth.

Weather

The **Equator** crosses South America near its widest part. Here, there are **tropical rain forests**. The weather is hot and rainy all year. There are grasslands north and south of the rainforest. It is hot and mainly dry there.

South America has the world's largest rainforest.

▲ *The Amazon River winds through the rainforest.*

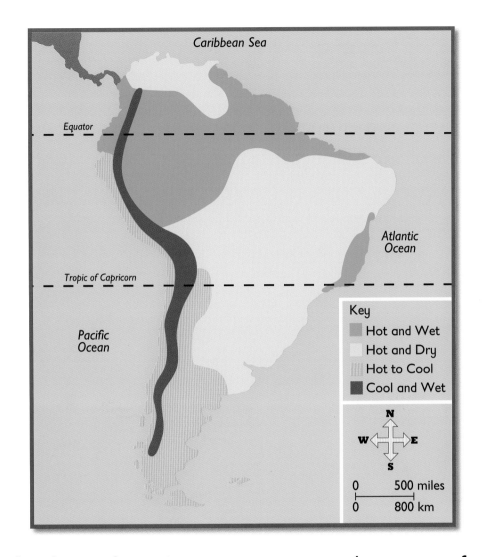

The high Andes Mountains are in the west of South America. They have cool and rainy weather. It is very cold and windy at the southern tip of South America.

Mountains and Deserts

The Andes mountain **range** is in South America. It is the longest mountain range in the world. There are hundreds of **volcanoes** in the Andes. Some still **erupt** today. The tallest peak is Mount Aconcagua, in Argentina.

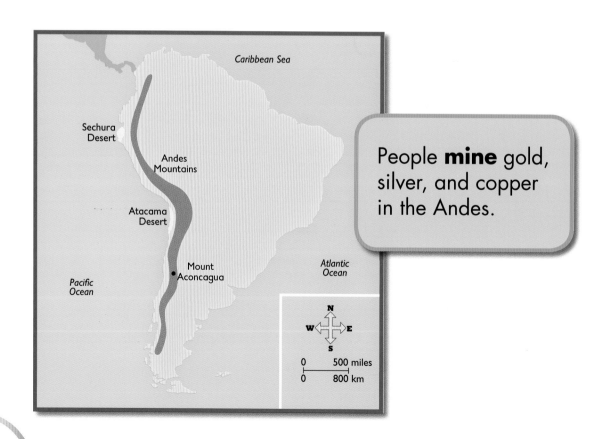

Caribbean Sea

Sechura Desert

Andes Mountains

Atacama Desert

Mount Aconcagua

Pacific Ocean

Atlantic Ocean

N
W E
S

0   500 miles
0   800 km

People **mine** gold, silver, and copper in the Andes.

No rain has ever been recorded in parts of the Atacama Desert.

▲ *The Atacama Desert in Peru is very rocky.*

There are **deserts** on the west coast of South America. It never rains there. During the day, the temperature in these deserts can reach 122 °F (50 °C). But at night, it is bitterly cold.

Rivers

The Amazon is the second longest river in the world. It carries more water than any other river. It begins in an icy lake in the Andes Mountains. Then, it flows through dense **rain forest** to the Atlantic Ocean.

Angel Falls is the tallest waterfall in the world.

▲ *Angel Falls is in Venezuela.*

Angel Falls is a very tall waterfall in Venezuela. Water falls into a deep **gorge**. People use the energy from the water to create electricity.

Lakes

South America has many large lakes. Lake Titicaca is high in the Andes Mountains. Giant frogs live among the **reeds** at the edge. People make boats from the reeds and go fishing on the lake.

Lake Guatavita is also in the Andes. Many years ago, people believed that the Sun was born here. Before a new **ruler** was crowned, he had to sail to the center of the lake. He had to throw golden gifts to the gods in the water.

▲ *Lake Guatavita is in Colombia, in the Andes.*

Animals

High in the mountains, farmers keep llamas, vicuñas, and alpacas. These strong animals look like small camels. They provide milk and meat. Their **dung** is burned as fuel. People make their long, fine wool into clothes.

▲ *Alpacas carry grass in Peru.*

An anaconda can open its jaws wide enough to eat a whole goat.

▲ *An anaconda searches for prey.*

Thousands of creatures live in South America's **rain forests**. Parrots and monkeys live in the trees. Anacondas are one of the world's largest types of snakes. They wait in rivers to pounce on their **prey**.

Plants

▲ *Sap comes from a rubber tree.*

Hundreds of products come from the trees and plants of South America. Rubber is made from the **sap** of rubber trees. Chewing gum is made from another tree. Many medicines have been made from South American plants.

Chocolate is made from the seeds of the cacao tree. Cacao trees grow wild in the **rainforests**. Today, cacao is often grown on farms.

The people of South America were the first people to make chocolate.

▲ *Cacao trees grow in Brazil.*

Languages

This map shows the countries in South America. Most people in these countries speak Spanish or Portuguese. Around 500 years ago, explorers came from Spain and Portugal to live in South America.

▲ *The Yahua people live in Peru.*

The first people to live in South America were **Native Americans**. They had their own languages and traditions. The Yahua people in Peru still speak their own language.

Cities

This map shows the main cities of South America. Rio de Janeiro is in Brazil. It is the busiest **port** in South America. Rio is famous for its beautiful beaches and lively **festivals**.

Santiago is a beautiful city. It is the **capital** of Chile. It was built by Spanish **settlers** near the Andes Mountains. The people of Santiago made money from **mining** silver and copper.

▲ *This is a view of Santiago.*

São Paulo is the largest city in South America.

▲ *São Paulo, Brazil, is a busy port.*

São Paulo is a busy **port** on the southeast coast. It is also an important center for buying and selling coffee. São Paulo has many factories that make steel, chemicals, and televisions.

Quito is one of the highest cities in the world.

▲ *Quito is in Equador.*

Quito is built on the side of a **volcano**. It is the **capital** of Ecuador. Quito is one of the oldest cities in South America. About 500 years ago, it was the capital of an ancient kingdom ruled by the Inca people.

In the Country

In the **rain forests** of South America, most people live on rivers. Today, their way of life is in danger. Many trees are being cut down for **timber** or to clear land for farming.

Traveling by boat is the easiest way to get from one village to another.

▲ *Some houses by the Amazon River are on stilts.*

▲ *This house in Peru is built from clay.*

Houses with thick clay walls keep **herders** warm in the cold mountains. Near the rain forest, farmers grow coffee, cacao, and sugar beet. In the cooler south, people grow wheat. There are huge cattle ranches.

Famous Places

Tierra del Fuego is a group of rocky islands at the tip of South America. Its name means "land of fire" in Spanish. This is because explorers saw campfires on the islands. Tierra del Fuego is now a **national park** with penguins and seals.

The Inca people built this walled city over 500 years ago.

▲ *Machu Picchu is an ancient city in Peru.*

Machu Picchu is in the Andes Mountains. It stayed hidden from the rest of the world for hundreds of years. The city contained houses, palaces, and **temples**. There was also an observatory, where people could study the stars.

This statue is lit up at night. It can be seen from many miles away.

▲ *A statue looks over Rio de Janeiro.*

In Rio de Janeiro, a giant statue of Jesus looks down on the harbor. Many people in South America are **Christians**. The Spanish and Portuguese **settlers** built churches and cathedrals all over the continent.

Many people work in **mines** in South America. In Chile, miners dig up copper. In Peru, they mine silver. Gold, emerald, and salt are all mined in Colombia.

Even the statues in this church are carved from salt.

▲ *This church in Colombia is carved from a salt mine.*

Fast Facts

South America's longest rivers

Name of river	Length in miles	Length in kilometers	Countries	Where it ends
Amazon	4,000	6,437	Peru, Colombia, Brazil	Atlantic Ocean
Parana (River Plate)	2,484	3,998	Brazil, Argentina, Paraguay	Atlantic Ocean
Purus	2,100	3,379	Brazil, Peru	Amazon River
Madeira	2,103	3,239	Brazil	Amazon River

South America's highest mountains

Name of mountain	Height in feet	Height in meters	Country
Aconcagua	22,841	6,962	Argentina
Ojos del Salado	22,572	6,880	Chile
Bonete	22,546	6,872	Argentina
Mercedario	22,211	6,770	Argentina, Chile
Huascaran	22,205	6,768	Peru

South America's record breakers

South America's Amazon **rain forest** is the largest rain forest in the world.

The Amazon rain forest has more types of plants than any other forest in the world.

The Andes Mountains are the longest mountain **range** in the world. They stretch for over 4,474 miles.

The Atacama **Desert** in Chile and Peru is one of the driest places in the world.

Angel Falls in Venezuela has a longer drop than any other waterfall in the world. The water falls for 3,212 feet (979 meters).

Glossary

capital city where government leaders work

Christian person who follows the religion of Christianity

desert hot, dry land with little rain

dung droppings of large animals, such as horses or llamas

Equator imaginary circle around the exact middle of Earth

erupt to throw out rocks and hot ash

festival time when people celebrate something

gorge very deep river valley with steep, rocky sides

herder someone who looks after a group of animals

mine to dig up things from under Earth's surface. Also, the place where things are dug up.

national park area of wild land protected by the government

Native Americans first people to live in North and South America

port town or city with a harbor, where ships come and go

prey animal that is eaten by other animals

rain forest thick forest that has heavy rain all year round

range line of mountains that are connected to each other

reed type of tall grass

ruler person who rules a country, such as a queen or president

sap liquid from a plant or tree

settler person who comes to live in a country

temple place built to worship a god or goddess

timber cut-up wood used for making things

tropical hot, wet places near the Equator

volcano hole in the earth from which hot, melted rock is thrown out

More Books to Read

Lynch, Emma. *We're from Mexico*. Chicago: Heinemann Library, 2006.

Miles, Elizabeth. *Watching Tree Frogs in South America*. Chicago: Heinemann Library, 2006.

Royston, Angela. *Mountains*. Chicago: Heinemann Library, 2005.

Index